THE VOICE

THE VOICE

Selected Poems

of Robert Desnos

Translated by William Kulik

with Carole Frankel

A Mushinsha Book
Grossman Publishers

ACKNOWLEDGEMENTS: to Editions Gallimard for permission to reproduce translations of La Colombe de l'arche, Les grands jours du poète, Destinée arbitraire, Le suicide de nuit, A la faveur de la nuit, La voix de Robert Desnos, J'ai tant rêvé de toi, Jamais autre que toi, Passé le pont, Vie d'ébène, De la fleur d'amour et des chevaux migrateurs, 10 juin 1936, La ville de Don Juan, Hommes, Mi-route, Fête-Diable, Au bout du monde, Les hommes sur la terre, Contes de fée, Couchée, Aujourd'hui je me suis promené, Réflexions sur la poésie, Lettre à Youki, Couplets de la rue Saint-Martin, Couplet du verre de vin, Couplet du trottoir d'été, and Couplet du boucher from *Domaine Public* (1953); La voix, Le cimetière, Le sort, La moisson, Le paysage, and La ville from *Contrée* (1962); and Une étoile filante from *Cinéma* (1966), all of which are © Editions Gallimard; to Editions Seghers for permission to reproduce translations of Mais je ne fus pas compris, 3/5/36, 5/5/36, 6/5/36, Tu prends la première rue à droite, Au temps des donjons, and Sol de Compiègne from *Robert Desnos,* by Pierre Berger, number 16 in *Poètes d'aujourd'hui* (1965); and to Doctor Michel Fraenkel for permission to reproduce translations of Rencontre and Le Veilleur du Pont-au-change. The illustrations are based on drawings by Robert Desnos.

First published in the United States of America in 1972
By GROSSMAN PUBLISHERS, 625 Madison Avenue,
New York City, 10022

Designed and produced by Mushinsha Limited, IRM/Rosei Bldg., 4, Higashi Azabu 1-chome, Minato-ku, Tokyo, Japan. Copyright in Japan, 1972, by Mushinsha Limited. All rights reserved. Printed in Japan.

First Edition 1972. Library of Congress Catalog Card No. 72–79579

INTRODUCTION

For much of his life, to Robert Desnos writing meant transmitting the "arbitrary fragments" of the unconscious, where from birth to death his one great poem was being elaborated. In him, this elaboration began at an early age: at six he was covering the pages of his notebooks with strange drawings; at twelve he was doing wildly imaginative gouaches and aquarelles. By sixteen he was keeping a journal of his dreams and writing poems; by nineteen he was published. By twenty-two, in the company of such as Andre Breton, Paul Eluard, Philippe Soupault, and Benjamin Peret, he had become the foremost practitioner of the art of automatic writing: the unconscious evoked at will and the spoken results recorded immediately. Breton called him the leader in Surrealist experimentation, *le cavalier le plus avancé*, whose life and work assumed an oracular quality. Desnos, prophetic, optimistic, was always confident of having enough life—"enough to salt the Pacific Ocean," he says in an early poem—to finish all his many projects. At thirty-six he sees many more years and many more things ahead of him. In his letter from the camps, he tells Youki to be sure to tell Gallimard that as soon as he returns, he will give him the manuscript of a love story in an entirely new genre. And, at Buchenwald, so the story goes, he moved in and out of the ranks of a group of pathetic shadows marked for the gas chamber, reading their palms, predicting—as he always had for himself—love, happiness, good fortune, long life. He was one month short of his forty-fifth birthday when he died, of typhus, at Terezin, June 8, 1945.

Desnos was born July 4, 1900, spiritual kin, it is often said, both to Rimbaud and to an earlier resident of Desnos' childhood neighborhood, the Saint-Merri quarter, Nicholas Flamel, 14th century alchemist. Something of an *enfant terrible*, he left home and school at sixteen. Unlike Rimbaud, however, without the anger and the hatred. Desnos remained on good terms with both his parents; he seems—quite simply—to have wanted to be free. So he went to work for a druggist, lived in a small room, ate an occasional meal with his parents. All the while writing his poems, painting his strange paintings, recording his dreams. It is easy to see why young Desnos, passionate, intense, was attracted to Surrealism. He was a prototype of the New Man that Surrealism saw possible: free, flexible, generous, spontaneous, optimistic about the possibilities for mankind—and most of all—in touch with his unconscious. . . .

Desnos was working for the Bonnefon publishing house when he met Benjamin Peret, whom he prodded until Peret introduced him to Breton; and the well-documented *epoque des sommeils*, the automatic writing seances, begins in 1922. Picture Desnos at this time: it is he of the famous photograph in *Nadja*,

with the heavy, glazed look, the pouches under the eyes—which the Czech student, Josef Stuna, knew, and so recognized him as he lay dying of typhus at Terezin. He dozes, he speaks in poetry; while Breton, somewhere between awe and envy, furiously records everything. Later, it is Desnos lying awake, hugging his phantom lover, imagining her there in his tiny room without a lock on the door, recording her visitations in *Journal of an Apparition*, writing dark, feverish, fantastic poems about her, such as the famous, "I Have Dreamed of You So Much." It is the same Desnos, full of brilliant wit, writing *Langage Cuit* and *Rrose Selavy*, reducing language to the ultimate, systematic illogicality of the homynym, creating endless "plays on words,"[1] pursuing these *jeux* with the same thoroughness and intensity he brought to everything he did, especially during this period of Surrealist excitement and activity. Throughout the twenties, Desnos identified himself with the Surrealists, signing their manifestos, contributing to their publications, *Litterature* and *Révolution Surréaliste*. He became a familiar figure at their favorite cafes, Les Deux Magots and the Cyrano, living in an easy, Bohemian style—as much a part of the Surrealist "message" as any scandalous public act or aggressive manifesto. By day he worked for Baillere, as a bookkeeper in medical publications; later for *Le Soir*[2] where he published much of his cinema criticism; at night he lived the life of a dedicated avant-gardiste.

Eventually, however, Surrealist dogma—and the domination of Breton—became too restrictive, and Desnos broke with the Movement, excoriating Breton in a fine piece of satire which he called the *Third Surrealist Manifesto*. And with the publication in 1930 of his first collection of poems, *Corps et Biens*, summing up a decade of poetry writing, his "apprenticeship" under Surrealism was ended. Also ended was the style of writing which characterizes a number of the poems in *Corps et Biens*, a style which Breton bluntly called "narcissistic." Though Desnos would later judge harshly the poems he wrote in the early thirties, many of them are among his greatest: simple, direct, humane. Broadly speaking, if the poems of the twenties reveal a closed world, endlessly reflecting itself, then the poems of the thirties reveal an open one, reflected over the shoulder of the poet—who must turn and identify with what he sees. Here are the great "fraternal poems"— "Men," "Men on Earth," "Mid-Way;" here are pure, delicate love poems—"Fairy Tale" and "June 10, 1936." Here are poems as transparent as a pane of glass—"You Take the First Street," "Lying Down," "Today I Took A Walk." In the best of these poems, *le merveilleux*—that perfect conjunction of conscious and unconscious the Surrealists worked to achieve—is realized in an insight of enormous compassion. His touch is kind even in a poem such as "Don Juan's City," where the atmosphere is arid, sterile. The promise made in poems of the middle twenties such as "The Voice of Robert Desnos" and "Of the Flower of Love and the Wandering Horses" has finally been kept.

During this time, Desnos was living in newer, more comfortable quarters with a beautiful woman named Youki—the "mysterious woman" his poems seem to have prophecied. In 1932, his friend Paul Deharme got him a job in radio, where he spent the remaining seven years until the mobilization, writing commercials and making up slogans. He lived a relatively settled life, financially secure for the first time. Among his friends of this period were the great and the near-great: Jean-Louis Barrault, Picasso; Georges Hugnet, Eluard; Felix Labisse, Artaud. But he was getting tired of the old way of writing poetry.

In 1936, Desnos undertook an experiment: to write a poem a day every day of the year. With this project, he begins to move toward a greater concentration on form, and away from automatism. Writing in 1942, he attributes this shift of concern to his passionate involvement in the "almost mathematical" work of creating slogans for radio, work in which the demands of the form required a strict adherence to the rhythms of popular speech. And, at the same time that he was getting new poetic life by making his inspiration work within given limits, he was expressing dissatisfaction with the methods which, he says, created a "verbal fog" which obscured the architecture of many of his poems. After 1936, the year of the "forced poems," the year which amounted virtually to an "intellectual purge," he begins to feel that "it is not poetry which must be free, but the poet." It is the end of his belief in the unconscious as sole creative tool.

And the sonnets and the other tightly constructed poems of *Contrée* (1944), his last book of poems, bear this out. They are stark, almost glacial—compared with the lyrical outpourings of the twenties. In the background, perhaps, is Desnos' last critical work, *Reflections on Poetry*, which states that the aim of great poetry is "to wed common language, the most common, to an indescribable atmosphere, to sharp imagery." The poems of *Contrée* are almost classical. We are facing *Rrose Selavy* from the opposite pole. We are "beyond automatism;" we are "beyond Surrealism." We are in the domain where form determines, as much as the all-important "inspiration of the moment," what a poem shall be. It is no longer a question, for Desnos, of "poetry received" but of "poetry imposed." It is no longer a question of drifting off to become the medium of one's unconscious. In these late words, it is apparently the older man, the man who confessed to a mania for moralities, sitting in judgement on his younger self. And, at last, on Surrealism. . . .

It is the older man who was mobilized in 1939, captured by the Germans and returned to Paris. Joining the Resistance network, he was important in the operation of *Editions du Minuit*, the underground press. In 1942, his second collection of poems, *Fortunes*, appeared. Under the name of Valentin Guillois he published several pieces, notably the great *Watchman of the Pont-au-Change*. It is Desnos at his prophetic, optimistic best. Arrested by the Gestapo in February, 1944, he was sent first to Compiègne, later to Buchenwald. In 1945, with the Allied armies closing in, the Buchenwald prisoners were force-marched by the retreating S.S. to Terezin. In May, after the Allies had occupied the camp, Desnos was discovered by Josef Stuna. He spent his last days talking with Stuna and a nurse, Alena Teresova, about Paris, poetry, freedom.

xi

a note on the translations:

Two tendencies are apparent in Desnos' work from the very beginning: one is toward a formal, oratorical style, the other toward a common, colloquial one. Sometimes both tendencies appear in the same poem, the shift from one level to another creating the *surprise* which may be at the heart of Desnos' method, at least some of the time. Whenever possible, I have tried to translate at the level of language the poem seemed to demand. But my primary concern was to get the voice of the man to come across in English. Because what is heard in his poetry is a *human* voice. It is there in the poems that Breton, perhaps rightly so, called narcissistic; it is there in the poems Desnos himself came to dislike. It is there in the last poems, however formal they may seem. Where it speaks most clearly will be where a reader hears it best.

William Kulik
Philadelphia, 1971

xii

[1] He acknowledged his debt to Marcel Duchamp for the title *Rrose Selavy*, in a manner typical of the entire method:

                13. Rrose Selavy connait bien le marchand du sel.

[2] It was while working for the newspaper that he attended a convention of journalists in Havana and, always a fan of popular expression, whether in music, art, or language, brought back to Paris the first recordings of the rumba and Cuban dances.

CONTENTS

THE VOICE

BUT I WAS NOT UNDERSTOOD

What corolla have you hidden your thumbs in?
Muzzle and handcuff love
You keep me from counting the days.
But the nights, there isn't one you don't speckle.

A tidal wave is washing the houses.
Right now they are blue.
Mountain ridges where memory is cut in two;
each side going limp
spattering my eyes with orange.

The name of God is a well-polished copper plate
on the gate of heaven,

but wipe your hands before praying.

uncollected
1923

MEETING

On your way.
Evening raises its white stick above the walkers.
Cowhorns in evenings of plenty you sow terror on the boulevard.
On your way.
It is the scroll of the hour, bizarre, luminous.
Struggle to the death. The referee counts to 70.
The mathematician wakes up and says
"I was so hot!"
Supernatural children dress like you and I.
Midnight adds a strawberry pearl to Madeleine's necklace
and then the doors of the station are slammed shut.
Madeleine, Madeleine, don't look at me that way
with peacocks flying out of your eyes.
The ashes of life are drying up my poem.
In the empty square invisible madness makes footprints in the wet sand.
The second boxer wakes up and says
"I was very cold."
Noon the hour of love delicately tortures
our sick ears.
A very wise doctor sews the hands of the praying woman
assuring her she will sleep.
An expert chef blends poisons on my plate
assuring me I will laugh.
I certainly will laugh.
The pointed sun, hair is called romance
    in the language I speak with Madeleine.
A dictionary gives the meaning of proper names:
Louis means roll of the dice,
Andre means reef,
Paul means etc. . . .
but your name is dirty:
                On your way!

1922
C'est les bottes de 7 lieues Cette phrase "Je me vois" (1923)

DOVE IN THE ARCH

Cursed!
be the father of the bride
of the blacksmith who forged the iron for the axe
with which the woodsman hacked down the oak
from which the bed was carved
in which was conceived the great-grandfather
of the man who was driving the carriage
in which your mother met your father.

November 14, 1923
Langage Cuit (1923)

21

THE GREAT DAYS OF THE POET

The disciples of light have never invented anything but
    not very heavy darkness.
The river rolls the body of a little woman and that means
    the end is near.
The widow in a wedding gown gets into the wrong procession.
We'll all arrive late at the grave.
A ship of flesh is swallowed by the sand of a little beach.
    The helmsman invites the passengers to be quiet.
The waves wait impatiently. Nearer, my God, to Thee!
The helmsman invites the waves to speak. They speak.
Night seals its bottles with stars and makes a fortune
    in the export trade.
Huge stores are built to sell nightingales.
    But they can't satisfy the desires of the
    Queen of Siberia who wants a white nightingale.
An English commodore swears he'll never again be caught
    picking sage at night between the feet of salt statues.
A propos of this a little Cerebos salt shaker gets up
    with difficulty on its delicate legs.
It pours what is left of my life onto my plate.
Enough to salt the Pacific Ocean.
Put a lifebuoy on my grave.
Because you never know.

C'est les bottes de 7 lieues Cette phrase "Je me vois"

ARBITRARY FATE

The time of the crusades is coming.
Through the closed window the birds insist on speaking
like fish in an aquarium.
In the window of a shop
a pretty woman is smiling.
Happiness, you're only sealing-wax
And I vanish like a will-o-the-wisp.
A great many keepers are chasing
a harmless butterfly escaped from the asylum.
In my hands it becomes a pair of lace pants
and your eagle-flesh
o my dream when I stroke you!
Tomorrow we will bury for free
we will no longer catch cold
we will speak the language of flowers
we will be enlightened by lights unknown to us now.
But today is today.
I feel my beginning is near
like the corn in June.
Police, pass me your handcuffs.
Statues turn away without obeying.
I will write insults on their pedestals and the name of my worst enemy.
Down in the ocean, underwater,
The body of a beautiful woman drives the sharks away.
They climb to the surface, are mirrored in the open air,
and do not dare gnaw those breasts,
those delicious breasts.

C'est les bottes de 7 lieues Cette phrase "Je me vois"

23

THE SUICIDE OF NIGHT

The green boughs dip when the dragonfly appears
    at the turn in the path
I approach a tombstone more transparent than snow
    white as milk as whitewash
    white as walls
The dragonfly wallows in the pools of milk
The glass armor shakes quivers moves forward
Rainbows are tied à la Louis Quinze
What? already the ground hidden by our path
    raises its hand
Struggles with the glass armor
Knocks at doors
Floats in the air
Cries out
Moans weeps aaaaaaaah! wake you are dying
    in this noise blue rock
Huge chunks of sponge falling from the sky
    cover the graveyards
Wine flows with a thunderous noise
The milk the hidden ground the armor struggle on the grass
    which reddens and whitens by turns
The thunder and the lightning and the rainbow
Ah! wake you crack you sing!

The little girl goes off to school reciting her lesson.

Les Ténèbres (1927)

IN THE KINDNESS OF NIGHT

To glide into your shadow in the kindness of night.
To follow your footsteps, your shadow at the window.
That shadow at the window is you and no one else;
it is you.
Do not open that window behind whose curtains you move.
Shut your eyes.
I would like to shut them with my lips.
But the window opens and the breeze, the breeze
which strangely balances flame and flag surrounds my escape
with its cloak.
The window opens: it is not you.
I knew it all along.

À la Mystérieuse (1926)

THE VOICE OF ROBERT DESNOS

So like a flower and a current of air
the flow of water fleeting shadows
the smile glimpsed at midnight this excellent evening
so like every joy and every sadness
it is the midnight past lifting its nude body
  above belfries and poplars
I call to me those lost in the fields
old skeletons young oaks cut down
scraps of cloth rotting on the ground and linen
  drying in farm country
I call tornadoes and hurricanes
storms typhoons cyclones
tidal waves
earthquakes
I call the smoke of volcanoes and the smoke of cigarettes
the rings of smoke from expensive cigars
I call lovers and loved ones
I call the living and the dead
I call gravediggers I call assassins
I call hangmen pilots bricklayers architects
assassins
I call the flesh
I call the one I love
I call the one I love
I call the one I love
the jubilant midnight unfolds its satin wings
  and perches on my bed
the belfries and the poplars bend to my wish
the former collapse the latter bow down
those lost in the fields are found in finding me
the old skeletons are revived by my voice
the young oaks cut down are covered with foliage
the scraps of cloth rotting on the ground and in the earth
  snap to at the sound of my voice like the flag of revolt
the linen drying in farm country clothes adorable women
  whom I do not adore

who come to me
obeying my voice, adoring
tornadoes revolve in my mouth
hurricanes if it is possible redden my lips
storms roar at my feet
typhoons if it is possible ruffle me
I get drunken kisses from the cyclones
the tidal waves come to die at my feet
the earthquakes do not shake me but fade completely
    at my command
the smoke of volcanoes clothes me with its vapors
and the smoke of cigarettes perfumes me
and the rings of cigar smoke crown me
loves and love so long hunted find refuge in me
lovers listen to my voice
the living and the dead yield to me and salute me
    the former coldly the latter warmly
the gravediggers abandon the hardly dug graves
    and declare that I alone may command their nightly work
the assassins greet me
the hangmen invoke the revolution
invoke my voice
invoke my name
the pilots are guided by my eyes
the bricklayers are dizzied listening to me
the architects leave for the desert
the assassins bless me
flesh trembles when I call

the one I love is not listening
the one I love does not hear
the one I love does not answer.

December 14, 1926
Les Ténèbres

NEVER ANYONE BUT YOU

Never anyone but you despite stars and loneliness
Despite the trees mutilated at nightfall
Never anyone but you will follow her path which is mine
The further you go the bigger your shadow gets
Never anyone but you will greet the ocean at dawn when I,
    worn out with wandering, coming through dark forests
    and nettle bushes, walk towards the foam
Never anyone but you will put her hand on my forehead
    over my eyes
Never anyone but you, and I renounce lying and unfaithfulness
You may cut the rope of this anchored ship
Never anyone but you
The eagle imprisoned in a cage slowly gnaws on the patina
    of the copper bars
What a deception!
It's the Sunday marked by nightingales singing
    in the tender green woods the boredom of little girls
    staring at a cage a canary flutters around in while
    in the empty street the sun slowly moves its thin line
    along the hot sidewalk
We'll cross other lines
Never never anyone but you
And I alone alone alone like withered ivy in suburban gardens
    alone like glass
And you never anyone but you.

Les Ténèbres

I HAVE DREAMED OF YOU SO MUCH

I have dreamed of you so much that you lose your reality.
Is there still time to reach that living body and kiss
onto that mouth the birth of the voice so dear to me?
I have dreamed of you so much that my arms, accustomed
to being crossed on my breast while hugging your shadow,
would perhaps not bend to the shape of your body.
And, faced with the real appearance of what has haunted
and ruled me for days and years, I would probably
become a shadow.
O sentimental balances.
I have dreamed of you so much it is no longer right
for me to awaken. I sleep standing up, my body exposed to
all signs of life and love, and you
the only one who matters to me now, I would be less able
to touch your face and your lips than the face and the lips
of the first person who came.
I have dreamed of you so much, walked so much, spoken
and lain with your phantom that perhaps nothing more is left me
than to be a phantom among phantoms and a hundred times more shadow
than the shadow which walks and will joyfully walk
on the sundial of your life.

A La Mystérieuse

29

ACROSS THE BRIDGE

The door is shut on the idol of lead.
Now there's nothing to make people notice
    that lonely house.
Perhaps only the water suspects something
The clear autumn mornings the rope around the neck plunge
    into the river
Never again will the forget-me-not little dog of Syracuse
    call the Persian-eyed farmer's wife with its ominous cry
From the time of Philippe le Bel across the crystal forests
    a loud cry comes and beats against the ivy-covered walls
The door is shut
Be quiet ah be quiet let the cold water sleep its deep sleep
Let the fish dive down toward the stars
The wind from the giant bed where murmurs rest
    the sinister wind of metamorphoses rises
Death to the teeth death to the white sail death to the everlasting
    summit
Let her sleep I say let her sleep or else
    I swear the earth will break open
That it will be all over between the moss and the coffin
I didn't say that
I didn't say a thing
What did I say?
Please, let her sleep
Leave the great oaks around her bed alone
Don't drive that shy, crumbling daisy
    out of her bedroom
Please, let her sleep.

Les Ténèbres

EBONY LIFE

A frightening stillness will mark this day
And the shadow of streetlights and fire-alarms
    will exhaust the light
All things, the quietest and the noisiest, will be silent
The suckling brats will die
The tugboats the locomotives the wind will glide by
    in silence
We will hear the great voice which coming from far away
    will pass over the city
We will wait a long time for it
Then towards the glare of *Milord*
When the dust the stones the missing tears
    form the sun's robe on the huge deserted squares
We shall finally hear the voice.
It will growl at doors for a long while
It will pass over the town tearing up flags
    and breaking windowpanes.
We will hear it
What silence before it, but still greater the silence
    it will not disturb but will hold guilty
    will brand and denounce
Day of sorrows and joys
The day the day to come when the voice
    will pass over the city
A ghostly sea-gull told me she loved me
    as much as I loved her
That this great terrible silence was my love
That the wind which carried the voice was the great revolt
    of the world
And that the voice would look kindly on me.

Les Ténèbres

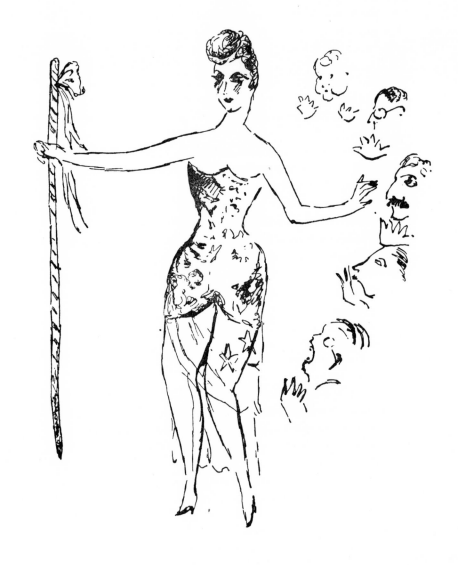

OF THE FLOWER OF LOVE
AND THE WANDERING HORSES

    In the forest there was a giant flower which risked killing
all the trees with her love
    The trees all loved her
    Towards midnight the oaks became reptiles and crept up
to her stem
    The ashes and the poplars bent down toward her corolla
The ferns yellowed in her soil
And she was more radiant than the nightly love
    of the sea and the moon.
More pale than the huge extinct volcanoes of this star
More sad and more nostalgic than the sand dried and soaked
    at the whim of the waves
I speak of the flower of the forest not of the tower
I speak of the flower of the forest and not of my love
And if such a flower, more pale and nostalgic and adorable,
    loved by the trees and the ferns, keeps my breath on her lips,
    it is because we are of the same essence
I met her one day
I speak of the flower and not of the trees
In the forest shuddering when I passed
Welcome butterfly who died in her corolla
And you rotting fern my heart
And you my eyes nearly ferns nearly coal nearly flame
    nearly wave
I speak in vain of the flower but of myself
The ferns have yellowed in the soil become like the moon
Like that exact instant in the agony of a bee lost
    between a cornflower and a rose and a pearl
The sky is not so closed
A man appears, chrysanthemum in his buttonhole, who gives his name
    and makes doors open
I speak of the impassive flower and not of the doors
    to adventure and solitude
One by one the trees died around the flower
Who profited by their decay

And that is why the plain became like the pulp of fruit
Why towns sprang up
A river at my feet winds and stops at my whim
　　　string of welcoming imagery
Somewhere a heart stops beating and the flower straightens up
The flower whose fragrance triumphs over time
　　　The flower which by itself revealed its existence to the plains
naked like the moon like the sea like the sterile atmosphere
of sad hearts
　　　A bright red lobster claw lies beside a pot
　　　The sun casts the shadow of the candle and the flame
　　　The flower straightens up with pride in a sky of invention
　　　Your nails my ladies are like its petals and red like them
　　　The forest murmuring low lays open
　　　A heart stopped like a dry spring
　　　There's no more time there's no more time to love you
who pass on your way
　　　The forest flower whose story I tell is a chrysanthemum
The trees are dead the fields have turned green towns have appeared
The great wandering horses paw the ground in their faraway stables
　　　Soon the great wandering horses leave
　　　The towns watch the herd pass through their streets
whose cobblestones ring with the clack of their hooves
and now and then glitter
　　　The fields are dug up by that cavalcade
　　　Tails dragging in the dust and nostrils smoking
they pass before the flower
　　　And for a long time their shadows remain
But what has become of the wandering horses whose speckled hides
　　　were promise of misery
Sometimes while digging in the earth someone comes across
　　　a strange fossil
It is one of their horseshoes
The flower which saw them still grows without blemish or weakness
　　　The leaves grow out along its stem
　　　The ferns blaze and bend toward the windows of houses
　　　But what has become of the trees
　　　The flower why does it flower
　　　Volcanoes! O volcanoes!
　　　The sky falls in
　　　I think of the faraway I think of the deepest within me

34

Vanished times are like nails broken on closed doors
　　　When in the country a peasant is going to die surrounded by
ripe fruit of the past season by the sound of frost cracking
on the windowpanes by boredom withered faded
like the cornflowers in the grass
　　　The wandering horses appear
　　　When a traveller loses his way in will-o-the-wisps
more broken than the lines in old people's foreheads and lies down
on the moving earth
　　　The wandering horses appear
　　　When a young girl lies naked at the foot of a birch and waits
　　　The wandering horses appear
　　　They appear in a gallop of broken bottles and grating cupboards
　　　They disappear into a hollow

No saddles have worn down their spines and their glistening rumps
　　　reflect the sky
They pass by spattering freshly plastered walls
And the frost cracking the ripe fruit the bare flowers the stagnant water
　　　and the soft earth of marshes slowly changing shape
See the wandering horses pass

　　　The wandering horses
　　　The wandering horses
　　　The wandering horses
　　　The wandering horses

Les Ténèbres

MEN

Men who grumble
Men of my two hands
Men of the early morning

The machine rolls at Deibler's command
And gear after gear in the odor of percolators
  that oozes out from under bar doors and the odor
  of hot croissants
The man who feels his socks stiffened by last night's sweat
and puts them on again
And his shirt stiffened by last night's sweat
and puts it on again
Who tells himself in the morning he'll wash up at night
And at night that he'll wash up in the morning
Because he's too tired . . .
And the one whose eyelids are glued together when he wakes up
And the one who wishes he had typhoid fever
So he could finally rest in his soft white bed . . .
And the emigrant who dines on nothing
While under his nose delicious scraps from the first class tables
are thrown into the sea
And the one who sleeps in the subway and is chased by the station master
  to the next station . . .

Men who grumble
Men of my two hands
Men of the early morning.

Les Sans Cou (1934)

DON JUAN'S CITY

Blind men, cripples, idiots
Hunchbacks, cops and drunks
Shuffling along.

Escaping from café windows
Enough steam to move a hundred ships.
The seven o'clock sirens cried in unison: "Time to get drunk."

Don Juan stopped at a place
Where I know there's a drinking-fountain
A fire-alarm and a wheelbarrow chained to a bench.

He stayed there until midnight,
He stayed there without getting bored,
Alone in the night.

At midnight, a woman in mourning
But naked under the huge veil on her hat
Appeared from a side street.

She was carrying a bottle of wine and a glass,
She was carrying a dead bird
She gave him the dead bird and a glass of wine.

A carriage door opened suddenly
A pretty girl with beautiful legs jumped out
And gave him her doll and a necklace of ebonies.

At a lighted window,
A woman was getting undressed
Throwing the hero the various pieces of her clothing.

The flower-lady on the corner
Brought him all her roses
And a hag selling papers all her papers.

A very beautiful very repulsive woman
Showed him her watch
And told him it didn't work any more.

A woman wearing wooden shoes, a peddler,
Came, holding up her apron.
In it, a fish like no other in the world.

She threw it in the gutter,
And the fish flopped around
Till it died.

The woman who won at baccarat,
The woman who just gave all her diamonds
        to her lover,
Came, too, through the streets and out of doors.

He brought some of them down from the sky
Like exhausted larks
He brought others up through the airholes in caves.

Some could have ruled empires
Others had filthy bodies and filthy minds.
Still others were carriers of dread diseases.

But Don Juan smelled an icy, refreshing wind
In the breath of the next morning,
A wind smelling of low tide and oysters

Which blew in his leaves and his branches,
And his roots sucked hungrily at the sweets
Of earth, however poor it was.

His bark was tougher than armor-plate,
Beating stronger than an athlete's heart,
And he wasn't cramped in his iron corset.

He helped the lamplighter,
The city sprinklers,
The garbage collectors and the postmen on their daily rounds.

For a handsome tree, he was a handsome tree.
They cut him down the following day,
They burned him and yet,

Yet his bitter sap was potent
And so many lovely women
Had walked under his leaves

That something of him remained
In the fireplace when his ashes cooled,
In the very hole where he had been.

To tell the truth, there's nothing much left of him,
A hole in the sidewalk,
A hole, nothing but an empty hole, a tiny hole.

Les Sans Cou

MID-WAY

There's a precise moment in time
When a man reaches the exact middle of his life.
A fraction of a second
A fleeting bit of time, quicker than a glance
Quicker than a fit of passion,
Quicker than light.
And a man is aware of this moment.

Long avenues with overhanging trees stretch out
Towards a tower where a lady sleeps
Whose beauty resists kisses, the seasons,
Like a star the wind, like a rock the waves.

A quivering boat sinks bawling.
A flag blows at the top of a tree.
A well-dressed woman with stockings fallen to her ankles
Appears on a street corner
Flushed, trembling,
Protecting with her hand an old-fashioned lamp which is smoking.

And in addition a drunken stevedore sings in the corner of a bridge
And in addition a mistress bites the lips of her lover
And in addition a rose petal falls on an empty bed
And in addition three clocks toll the same hour
At several minute intervals
And in addition a man passing in the street comes back
Because someone has called his name
But it is not he this woman is calling.
And in addition a public official in full dress
Cramped by his shirttail wedged
      between his pants and his underwear
Dedicates an orphanage
And in addition a wonderful tomato falls from a truck speeding
Through the empty streets and rolls into the gutter
To be swept away later
And in addition a fire breaks out on the seventh floor of a building
And burns in the heart of the silent and indifferent city

And in addition a man hears a long forgotten song
which he will forget again
And in addition many other things
Many other things a man sees at the precise moment of the middle of his life
Many other things happen for a long time
        in the briefest of brief instants on earth.
He ponders the mystery of that second, that fraction of a second,

But he says, "Let's get rid of dark thoughts"
And he gets rid of them.
And what could he say?
And what better could he do?

Les Sans Cou

MEN ON EARTH

There were four of us at a table
Drinking red wine and singing
When we felt like it.

A wallflower fades in a garden gone to seed
The memory of a dress at the bend of an avenue
Venetian blinds beating against a sash.

The first man says: "The world is wide and the wine is fine
Wide is my heart and fine my blood
Why are my hands and my heart so empty?"

A summer evening the chant of rowers on a river
The reflection of huge poplars
And the foghorn from a tug requesting passage.

The second man says: "I discovered a fountain
The water was fresh and sweet-smelling
I no longer know where it is and all four of us are dying."

How beautiful are the streams in small towns
On an April morning
When they carry rainbows along.

The third man says: "We were born a short time ago
And already we have more than a few memories
Though I want to forget them."

A stairway full of shadow
A door left ajar
A woman surprised naked.

The fourth man says: "What memories?
This moment we are camped
And my friends we are going to leave one another."

Night falls on a crossroad
The first light in the fields
The odor of burning grass.

We left each other, all four of us
Which one was I and what did I say?
It was a long long time ago.

The glistening rump of a horse
The cry of a bird in the night
The rippling of water under a bridge.

One of the four is dead
Two others are hardly better off
But I am doing well and I think it will last for a long while.

The hillsides covered with thyme
The ancient mossy courtyard
The old street that led to the forest.

Men, life, friendships reborn,
And the blood of the whole world circulating in veins,
In many different veins but in the veins of men,
     of men on earth.

Les Portes Battantes (1936)

43

DEVIL-FEAST

The last drop of wine flares up at the bottom of the glass
    where a castle has just appeared.
Gnarled trees at the edge of the road lean down towards the traveler.
He comes from the town nearby,
He comes from the city far away,
He simply passes by the foot of steeples.
He sees a red star moving in a window
Which comes down, which walks wavering
On the white road into the black country.
It steers toward the traveler who watches it approach.
For an instant it shines in his eyes,
It settles on his forehead.
Stunned by the cold gleam which lights him up,
He wipes his forehead.
A drop of wine beads on his finger.
Now the man moves off and grows tiny
    in the night.
He has passed near the spring where you come in the morning
    to pick watercress,

He has passed near the abandoned house.
He is the man with the drop of wine on his forehead.
At this moment he is dancing in a huge room,
A brilliantly lit room
Its waxed parquet floor glistening
Deep as a mirror.
He is alone with his partner
In that huge room, and he dances
To the music of an orchestra of ground glass.
And the creatures of night
Gaze at this one couple dancing
And the most beautiful of the creatures of night
Mechanically wipes a drop of wine from his forehead,
Puts it back into a glass,
And the sleeper awakes,
Sees the drop shining like a hundred thousand rubies in the glass
Which was empty when he fell asleep.
Gazes at it.
The universe quivers during a second of silence
And sleep reclaims its rights,
And the universe resumes its course
Along the millions of white paths traced throughout the world
Across the dark fields.

Les Sans Cou

45

AT THE END OF THE WORLD

That mouthing off in the black street at whose end
the river shudders against its banks.
That butt thrown from a window forms a star.
That mouthing off again in the black street.
Ah! Shut yours!
Oppressive, stifling night.
A cry approaches, almost touching,
but it dies at the very moment it reaches us.

Somewhere in the world, at the foot of an embankment,
a deserter pleads with sentries
who do not understand his language.

Les Portes Battantes

MAY 3, 1936

The river a shower torments at dawn
Reflects the glittering scales of fish
water bubbles, fragments of glass, the bodies of dead dogs
in the course of the waters, in the course of our days
        endlessly turning.

uncollected

MAY 5, 1936

Undress
bathe in that dark pond
You have nothing to fear
You've done it before
Your waterproof body doesn't absorb like a sponge

The sun will dry the mud
It will fall into dust
bathe
go ahead
The earth is vast and so is your heart
which, all things carefully considered,
has not yet known error
and has never known mud.

uncollected

MAY 6, 1936

Have I really lived for thirty-six years?
It isn't even yesterday that my memories
my dreams my loves occurred
it is today
The balcony on rue Saint-Martin
the shop where I looked at the dusty sponges
The temples on the quai
All that is still there
but above everything
I sense many more years
And many more things
ahead of me.

uncollected

49

JUNE 10, 1936

At the bend in the road
He reached out his hand
To the beautiful morning.

The sky was so clear
That the clouds
Looked like foam on the sea.

And blossoms on the apple trees
Turned white in meadows
Where wash was hung out to dry.

The spring which sang
Sang of the life which passed
Along the meadows and the hedgerows.

And the distant forest
Where the grass was turning green
Was full of bell-like sounds.

Life was so beautiful
It entered his eyes
His heart and his ears so completely,

That he broke out laughing:
He laughed at the world and at the sighing
Wind in the flowering trees.

He laughed at the way the earth smelled,
He laughed at the wash of the washerwomen,
He laughed at the clouds passing overhead.

As he was laughing on a hilltop,
A girl with a beautiful face appeared
From a house nearby.

And the girl laughed too
And when her laughter vanished
The birds began to sing again.

She laughed to see him laugh
And the doves mirrored
In the still waters of a pond
Heard her laughter vanish in the air.

They never saw each other again.

She often went along the road
Where the man held out his hand
To the morning light.

Many times he remembered her
And the all too clear memory
Could be seen in his eyes.

Many times she remembered him
And saw his face
In the dark water of a well.

One by one the years passed
Turning pale like the cards a player holds
In his hands as dawn breaks.

Both are rotting in the earth
Chewed by the honest worms.
The earth fills their mouths to keep them quiet.

They might call out to each other at night
If death weren't so horrified by the sound:
The road is there and time passes.

But every day a beautiful morning
Falls like an egg into the hand
Of someone passing along the road.

Every day the sky is so clear
That the clouds
Are like foam on the sea.

Dead people! Dark wrecks in the earth,
We don't know your miseries
The hermits sing of.

We swim, we are alive,
In the innocent air of each season.
Life is beautiful and the air is good.

Les Portes Battantes

FAIRY TALE

Many times upon a time
There was a man who loved a woman.
Many times upon a time
There was a woman who loved a man.
Many times upon a time
There was a man and there was a woman
Who did not love the ones who loved them.

Once upon a time
Perhaps only once
A man and a woman who loved each other.

uncollected

A SHOOTING STAR

One lovely summer evening a shooting star appears in the sky. It passes over a town and is seen by a girl on a balcony who makes a wish: "to be loved, to be loved forever." It passes over a crossroads where a young man also makes a wish: "to love, to love forever." It passes over an orchard where a girl makes another wish, the third: "never to love."

And, naturally, the three characters meet during a dance at a country festival. Naturally the young man will fall in love with the second girl, who will not love him. The first girl will be alone. It is she who will become the young man's confidante.

Finally, the young man will succeed in marrying the one he loves, and life goes on, sad for the unloved lover, empty for the woman who does not love, dismal for the one who wants to be loved and is not. The drama becomes more and more entangled around the three characters, because as time goes by, the man sees his desires crystallizing, bit by bit, in his confidante. The action will go on building up to the day when, during a fire, the young man will choose to save, not his wife, but the woman who wants to be loved.

Above the smoking ruins a shooting star will prompt their last wish: "to love each other."

Around this scenario must be a town, the work of the fields, the procession of the seasons, the aging of the world.

uncollected scenario

54

YOU TAKE THE FIRST STREET

You take the first street on the right
You follow the quai
You cross the bridge
You knock at the door of the house.

The sun shines
The river runs
In a window a pot of geraniums trembles
A car goes by on the opposite shore.

You turn back to the cheerful scene
Without seeing that the door has opened behind you
The hostess stands on the threshold
The house is full of shadow.

But on the table is the reflection
The reflection of the daylight on a piece of fruit and a bottle
On a china plate and a piece of furniture
And you stand there on the threshold between the
World full of people like yourself
And your droning solitude of the entire world.

uncollected

LYING DOWN

On my right, the sky, on my left, the sea.
And in front of me, grass and flowers.
A cloud moves along vertically,
Parallel to the plumb-line horizon,
Parallel to a man on horseback.
The horse runs to its doom
While the cloud climbs endlessly.
How simple and strange everything is.
Lying on my left side,
I lose interest in the landscape
And think only of very vague things,
Vague and very pleasant,
Like the weary look that is turned,
This beautiful summer afternoon,
To the left, to the right,
Here and there,
In a frenzy of the useless.

uncollected

TODAY I TOOK A WALK . . .

Today I took a walk with my friend
Even though he's dead,
I took a walk with my friend.

How beautiful the flowering trees,
The chestnut trees which snowed the day of his death.
With my friend I took a walk.

Long ago my parents
Went alone to funerals
And I felt like a small child.

Now I know a good many dead men
I've seen a lot of undertakers
But I don't get too close to them.

That's why all day today
I took a walk with my friend.
He found me aged a little,

Aged a little but he said:
Some day you too will be where I am,
One Sunday or Saturday.

And I looked at the flowering trees,
At the river passing under the bridge
And suddenly I saw I was alone.

So I came back among the living.

1936
(published in *État de Veille*, 1942)

VERSES ON THE BUTCHER

If you like, lovely lady, I'll make your bed
in the bloody decor of my shop.
My knives will be the magic mirrors
Where the day dawns, shines and grows pale.
I'll make your bed deep and warm
In the open belly of a heifer
And, while you're having your beauty sleep
I'll watch over it like a hangman on a scaffold.

État de Veille

VERSES ON THE SUMMER SIDEWALK

Let's lie down on the pavement
Warmed by the sun, washed by the sun,
In the good smell of dust
At the close of day,
Before the risen night,
Before the first light,
And we'll watch in the gutter for
Reflections of the clouds ready to attack
The bloody fit of the horizon
And the first star above the houses.

État de Veille

VERSES ON THE GLASS OF WINE

When the train is leaving, don't wave your hand,
Or your handkerchief, or your umbrella,
Instead, fill a glass with wine
And throw the long flame of the wine
At the train with its singing siderails,
The flame of wine bloody like your tongue
And sharing with it
The palate and the couch
Of your lips and your mouth.

État de Veille

VERSES ON RUE ST-MARTIN

I don't like rue Saint-Martin any more
Since Andre Plattard left it.
I don't like rue Saint-Martin any more,
I don't like anything, not even wine.

I don't like rue Saint-Martin any more
Since Andre Plattard left it.
He's my friend, he's my buddy,
We split room and board.
I don't like rue Saint-Martin any more.

He's my friend, he's my buddy,
He disappeared one morning
They took him away, no one knows any more.
He hasn't been seen again in rue Saint-Martin.

Don't bother praying to the saints,
Saints Merri, Jacques, Gervais and Martin,
Not even Valerien, hidden on the hill.
Time goes by, no one knows a thing.
Andre Plattard left rue Saint-Martin.

État de Veille

THE TOWN

To run into the crowd through the streets,
Seized in broad daylight by anguish and fear,
To sense danger death and sorrow,
To cover up his tracks and run from shadows barely glimpsed,

Is the fate of a man who, dreaming on his way,
Gets lost in his dreams and mingles with phantoms,
Glides along in their coat, takes their place in the kingdom
Where matter gives way to the caress of hands.

He invented it all in his head.
Surrounding, disguising, betraying, clutching,
He must stop, let the train of creatures
Born in his reeling body pass.

Vomit of memories, regrets of widowed suns,
Springs bubbling up, echo of an obscure song,
You are nothing but scum, nothing but foam.
I would like to be born each day under a new sky.

Contrée (1944)

FATE

I have wished for your death and nothing can keep it
    from coming prematurely
I have seen you covered with sweat and pus
At the very height of your agony
And everything in you was cruel and insane.

Listen. That day a thick cloud rose from the hills
    of Bicetre
And climbed up behind the Dome du Val-de-Grace.
A new-born child cried out,
Rue St-Jacques, in a run-down house.

From now on nothing can save you from shame and misery
For my wish had the taste of things which come to pass.
Already hidden physical signs, in your mind
    and in your heart,
Warn you it is time and goodbye to the suitcase.

It is no use weeping and repenting,
No use being noble,
For nothingness is your only becoming
And your name will not survive in popular proverbs.

The dark cloud passed Val-de-Grace and Saint Sulpice,
For a long time it was reflected in the Seine before
    dissolving into storm.
And I watched it from the top of a white building
And its thunder liberated huge birds from their cage.

Contrée

HARVEST

It is unthinkable to think of yourself
Alive, real, existing.
It is unthinkable to think of yourself
Dead, deceased, defunct, outside of time.
It is unthinkable to think of yourself
And still more unthinkable
To think of yourself as a memory,
A dream, a soul without a body.

Beautiful roses of the past,
Roses, fragrant roses
Which tremble after dawn,
By night already opened wide,
Your fate, brief and long,
Is the same as our years
Even if, in the drawing room,
You are brought in faded.

Our gods were too fragile.
They were little people
In a little house
Living on very little money.
Our fortune is greater
And our fate more gloomy.
We do not want the moon.
We do not fear our death.

Tied firmly by the five senses
Our universe shrinks.
Goodbye dream, goodbye beauty!
I sacrifice you
To the too limited world.

Contrée

THE LANDSCAPE

I had dreamed of loving. I still love but love
Is no longer that bouquet of lilacs and roses
Filling the woods with their fragrance
Where a flame lies at the end of paths which do not bend.

I had dreamed of loving. I still love but love
Is no longer that storm where the lightning superimposes
Its pyres on castles, routs, convulses, illuminates,
While fleeing the parting of the ways.

It is the spark of flint under my footstep at night,
The word no dictionary in the world has translated
The foam on the sea, that cloud in the sky.

With age all becomes rigid and clear,
Streets without names, ropes without knots.
I feel myself harden with the landscape.

Contrée

THE CEMETERY

My grave will be here and nowhere else, under these three trees.
I pick from them the first leaves of spring
Between a pedestal of granite and a marble column.

I pick from them the first leaves of spring,
But other leaves will feed on the auspicious rot
Of this body which will live, if it may, a hundred thousand years.

But other leaves will feed on the auspicious rot,
But other leaves will blacken
Under the pen of those who tell their tales.

But other leaves will blacken
From an ink more fluid than blood and the water of fountains:
Unexecuted wills, words lost beyond the mountains.

From an ink more fluid than blood and the water of fountains
Can I defend my memory against oblivion
Like a squid fleeing, running out of blood, running out of breath?

Can I defend my memory against oblivion?

Contrée

66

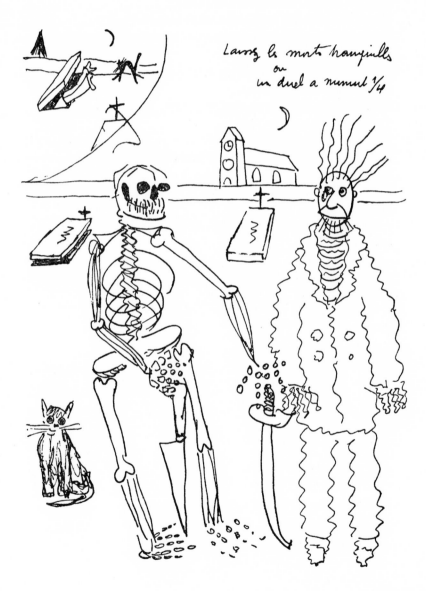

Laissez les morts tranquilles
ou
un duel a minuit 1/4

TIME OF THE DUNGEONS

Have you forgotten the password already?
The castle is closed and becomes a prison,
The beautiful lady on the battlements sings her song
And the prisoner moans in his chains.
Will you rediscover the path, the plain,
Source and sanctuary in the heart of the forests,
The bend in the river where dawn appeared,
The evening star and the full moon?
A forked serpent springs at man,
Entwining him, binding him in its coils,
The beautiful lady sighs on the edge of the battlements,
The setting sun glitters on the spears,
Time never to return springs at man,
Entwining him, binding him in its years.
Loves! Seasons! Faded beauties!
Serpents coiled in the underbrush.

État de Veille

THE WATCHMAN OF THE PONT-AU-CHANGE

I am the watchman of the rue de Flandre.
I watch while Paris sleeps.
Far to the north, fire lights up the night sky.
I hear planes flying over the city.

I am the watchman of the Point du Jour.
The Seine winds along in the darkness around the Auteuil Viaduct,
Under twenty-three bridges across Paris.
I hear bombs exploding to the west.

I am the watchman of the Porte Doree.
Shadows of the Vincennes forest thicken around the castle.
I have heard cries from the direction of Creteil
And trains rolling east in a wave of defiant singing.

I am the watchman of the Poterne des Peupliers.
The south wind brings me acrid smoke,
Vague murmuring and sounds of the dying
Which fade away in Plaisance or Vaugirard.

To the north, to the south, to east and west,
Nothing but the thunder of war converging on Paris.
I am the watchman of the Pont-au-Change
Awake in the heart of Paris in the growing roar
And I recognize the panicked nightmares of the enemy,
The victory shouts of the allies and the French,
The agonized screams of our brothers tortured by Hitler's Germans.

I am the watchman of the Pont-au-Change
Watching not only this night over Paris,
This stormy night not only over Paris in her fever and exhaustion,
But over the whole world which surrounds and crushes us.
In the crisp air all the sounds of war
Converge on this place where men have lived for so long.

Cries, songs, sounds of the dying, sounds of riot, they come from everywhere.
Victory, suffering and death, a sky the color of white wine and tea,

From the four corners of the horizon, across the barriers of earth,
With the scent of vanilla, of wet earth and blood,
Of salt water, with powder and funeral fires,
With kisses from an unknown giant sinking at each step into earth
slippery with human flesh.

I am the watchman of the Pont-au-Change
And I greet you on the threshold of the promised day,
All you my comrades from the rue de Flandre to the Poterne des Peupliers,
From Point du Jour to Porte Doree.

I greet you who sleep
After your dangerous secret work,
Printers, bomb-carriers, railyard-wreckers, incendiaries,
Distributors of tracts, smugglers, messengers,
I greet you who resist, twenty-year-olds with smiles as pure as springs,
Old men more venerable than bridges, strong men, images of the seasons,
I greet you on the threshold of the new morning.

I greet you on the banks of the Thames,
Comrades of all nations present at the meeting,
In the ancient English capital,
In ancient London, in ancient Britain.

Americans of all races and all flags,
Beyond the broad Atlantic,
From Canada to Mexico, from Brazil to Cuba,
Comrades from Rio, from Tehuantepec, from New York and San Francisco.
I have made a rendez-vous with the whole earth on the Pont-au-Change,
Watching and fighting like you. Just now,
Warned by his heavy, ringing footsteps,
I too have slaughtered my enemy.

He is dead in the gutter, this nameless Hitler German,
His face soiled with mud, his memory already rotting.
While I heard your voices from the four seasons,
Friends, friends and brothers of friendly nations.
I heard your voices in the scent of African orange trees,
In the heavy staleness of the Pacific,
White squadrons of hands held out in the darkness,
Men of Algiers, Honolulu, Chunking,

70

Men of Fez, of Dakar, of Ajaccio.

Terrifying and unnerving clamor, rhythms of lungs and hearts,
From the Russian front blazing in the snow,
From Lake Ilmen to Kiev, from the Dnieper to Pripet,
You come to me, born from millions of breasts.

I hear you and understand you, Norwegians, Danes, Hollanders,
Belgians, Czechs, Poles, Greeks, Luxemburgers,
Albanians and Yugoslavs, comrades of battle,
I hear your voices and I call to you,
I call to you in my language known to all
A language which has only one word:
Freedom!
And I tell you that I am watching and that I have slaughtered one of Hitler's men.
He is dead in the empty street.
In the heart of the unmoved city I have avenged my brothers assassinated
At the fort at Romainville and on Mt. Valerien,
In the fleeting reborn echoes of the world, the city and the seasons.

And others like me watch and kill,
Like me they lie in wait for ringing footsteps in deserted streets,
Like me they hear the chaos and the thunder of earth.

At Porte Doree, at Point du Jour,
Rue de Flandre and Poterne des Peupliers,
Across the whole of France, in the towns and in the fields,
My comrades wait for the steps in the night
And soothe their loneliness with the chaos and the thunder of earth.

For the earth is a camp lighted by thousands of fires.
On the eve of battle, watch is kept throughout the earth
And perhaps, comrades, you hear the voices,
The voices which come from here when night falls,
Which tear at lips hungry for kisses
Which fly endlessly across great stretches
Like migratory birds blinded by beacon lights
Smashing themselves against the fiery windows.

Let my voice come to you
Warm, joyful, and determined,

71

Without fear and without remorse,
Let my voice come to you with that of my comrades,
The voice of ambush and the French vanguard.

Listen to us in your turn, sailors, pilots, soldiers,
We wish you good morning,
We speak to you not of our suffering but of our hope,
On the threshold of the new day we wish you good morning,

To you who are near and, also, to you
Who will receive our morning prayer
At the moment when the early dawn enters your houses in straw boots.
Good morning just the same and good morning for tomorrow!
Good morning with full heart and with all our being!
Good morning, good morning, the sun is going to rise over Paris,
Even if the clouds hide it it will be there,
Good morning, good morning, with all my heart good morning!

published under the name Valentin Guillois—
Europe, Éditions de Minut

SOIL OF COMPIÈGNE

CHORUS (hurried and overlapping):
>   Chalk and flint and grass and chalk and flint
>   And flint and dust and chalk and flint
>   Grass, grass and flint and chalk, flint and chalk
>   (slowing):
>   Flint, flint and chalk
>   And chalk and flint
>   And chalk . . .

A VOICE:
>   Somewhere between l'Hay-les-Roses
>   And Bourg-la-Reine and Anthony
>   Between the roses of l'Hay
>   Between Clamart and Anthony

CHORUS (very rhythmical):
>   Chalk and flint—chalk and flint
>   And chalk
>   And flint and chalk and flint and chalk
>   And flint

A VOICE:
>   Between the roses of l'Hay
>   And the trees of Clamart
>   Have you seen the siren
>   The siren of Anthony
>   Who sang in Bourg-la-Reine
>   Who sings yet in Fresnes.

73

CHORUS:
>   Soil of Compiègne!
>   Rich yet barren earth
>   Earth of flint and chalk
>   We make footprints in your flesh
>   So that some day the spring rain
>   Might lie there like the eye of a bird
>   And reflect the sky, the sky of Compiègne
>   With your images and your stars
>   Heavy with memory and dream
>   Harder than flint
>   More yielding than chalk under a knife

A VOICE:
>   In Paris near Bourg-la-Reine
>   I left my loves alone
>   Ah! may the sirens lull them
>   I sleep tranquil, o my loves
>   And at l'Hay I gather roses
>   That I will one day bring you
>   Heavy with perfume and dream
>   And, like your eyelids, opened
>   To the bright sun of a life not so brief
>   Filled with flashes of lightning like a flintstone,
>   Luminous like chalk

CHORUS (staggered):
>   And chalk and flint and flint and chalk
>   Soil of Compiègne!
>   Soil made for walking
>   And the long stand of trees,
>   Soil of Compiègne!

74

Like all the soil of earth,
Soil of Compiègne!
One day we will shake our dust off
Onto your dust
And leave singing.

A VOICE:

We will leave singing
Singing to our loves
Life is short and short the time.

SECOND VOICE:

Nothing is more beautiful than our loves.

ANOTHER VOICE:

We will leave our dust
In the dust of Compiègne.
        (emphasizing each syllable):
And we will carry off our loves
Our loves may we remember them

CHORUS:

May we remember them.

published under the name Valentin Guillois

REFLECTIONS ON POETRY

There is a poetic constant. There are changes of fashion. There are changes of fad. There are also themes so overbearing that they must be expressed at any cost. These themes exist at this moment and they must be expressed at this moment.

*

Each person finds his poetic food where he likes. Reading *Dieux Verts* by Pierre Devaux has taught me more about a possible poetic technique than such and such a weighty essay.

*

Villon, Gerard de Nerval, Gongora, together with the great Baffo, seem to me subjects for current reflections concerning poetic technique. To wed common language, the most common, to an indescribable atmosphere, to sharp imagery; to annex domains which, even in our day, seem incompatible with that fiendish "noble language" which is endlessly reborn in languages ripped away from the mangy Cerebus which guards the entrance to the poetic domain, is what seems to me work worth doing, without forgetting, I repeat, certain overbearing themes of inspiration of the moment . . .

*

The greatest names of our time (I am speaking of poets) are still not assured of a prominent place on the third shelf of an inquisitive scholar of the year 2000. However, that isn't important. It may be that great poetry is necessarily of the present, from events . . . therefore it may be short-lived.

*

Poetry may be this or it may be that. But it shouldn't necessarily be this or that . . . except delirious and lucid.

*

Schools follow and get mixed up with each other. Romanticism now comprises the Parnassian school, symbolism, naturalism. There is an atheistic romanticism, a Catholic romanticism. And, looked at closely, Romanticism reconciles the philosophical 18th century and the metaphysical Middle Ages . . . like the cook making a salad who thought he could reconcile oil and vinegar.

*

It seems to me that beyond Surrealism there is something very mysterious to be dealt with, that beyond automatism there is the intentional, that beyond poetry there is the poem, that beyond poetry received there is poetry imposed, that beyond free poetry there is the free poet.

*

I feel that mysterious domain I just spoke of behind Nerval, whom it will be necessary to start out from again in order to be liberated from Mallarmé, Rimbaud and Lautréamont. Though perhaps the doors to this domain can only be opened with a word from the jargon ballads of Villon.

*

Gongora . . . the poem follows its perfectly straight path on a wide avenue across the dark, tufted forest; though to both left and right, little intersecting roads lead away, sinuous paths toward the edges, and Gongora doesn't leave that out, he keeps it, he absorbs it, he takes it away like a hunted fugitive who would take away with him the fields themselves and not the key to them. . . .

Paris, January 1944

77

LETTER TO YOUKI

March 28
and
July 15, 1944

My love,

Our suffering would be unbearable if we couldn't think of it as a passing and sentimental illness. Our rediscoveries will adorn our life for at least thirty years. As for me, I'm taking a deep drink of youth, and I'll come back to you full of love and strength! During our separation a birthday, my birthday was the occasion of a long fantasy about you. Will my letter reach you in time for your birthday? I would have liked to give you 100,000 American cigarettes, a dozen dresses from the great couturiers, an apartment on the rue Seine, a car, the cottage in the Compiègne forest, the one on Belle-Isle and a little four-sous bouquet. While I'm gone, keep flowers around constantly; I'll pay you back for them. All the rest, I promise it to you later.

But above everything, drink a bottle of good wine and think of me. I hope our friends won't forget to visit you that day. I thank them for their courage and their devotion. About a week ago I got a package from J-L Barrault. Kiss him for me, and Madeleine Renaud, too; the package is proof that my letter got through. I haven't gotten an answer; I'm waiting every day for one. Kiss everyone in the family, Lucienne, Aunt Juliette, Georges. If you run into Passeur's brother, give him my best and ask him whether he knows anyone who can help you if you need it. What is happening with my books at the printer's? I have many ideas for poems and novels. I regret having neither freedom nor time to write them. But you can tell Gallimard that within three months after I get back he'll have the manuscript of a love story in an entirely new genre. I'm ending this letter for today.

Today, July 15th, I got four letters, from Barrault, Julia, Dr. Benet and Daniel. Thank them and apologize for me for not answering. I'm allowed only one letter a month. Still no word from you, but they send me news of you; that will be for next time. I hope that letter is our life to come. My love, I embrace you as tenderly as propriety allows in a letter which has to pass the censor. A thousand kisses. Have you gotten the little trunk I sent to the hotel in Compiègne?

Robert

Buchenwald

THE VOICE

A voice, a voice from so far away
It no longer makes the ears tingle.
A voice like a muffled drum
Still reaches us clearly.

Though it seems to come from the grave
It speaks only of summer and spring.
It floods the body with joy.
It lights the lips with a smile.

I listen. It is simply a human voice
Which passes over the noise of life and its battles
The crash of thunder and the murmur of gossip.

And you? Don't you hear it?
It says "The pain will soon be over"
It says "The happy season is near."

Don't you hear it?

Contrée